TINKER

How Smart Business Owners Develop Creative Ideas for True Growth

Dear Kathy,
Trust your hunches —
That's where the
magic starts !
Susan

SUSAN TRIVERS

TABLE OF CONTENTS

FOREWORD
BY
MARK LEBLANC

In your hands you hold a *street smart* book written by a wise author. Susan Trivers is rare indeed. Her experience and depth of expertise in business make her uniquely qualified to share her wisdom and insights.

I have been on my own nearly my entire adult life. Over the least 35 years, I have had my share of the good, bad, ugly and the great. I have had my share of periods where I felt stuck, stagnant or simply stalled out. Here is where Susan delivers.

She is the consummate pro when it comes to focus and creativity. Her philosophy revealed in Tinker is a model for unlocking a new combination for accelerated growth. Often we are so close to success we cannot see it. Changing it up or trying a new approach can be the difference between ordinary results and extraordinary success.

Many entrepreneurs and business owners are at risk today due to a lack of creativity or simply the busyness of business. Tinker gives you permission to try a new idea or take an idea and breathe new life into it. You will never know what lies ahead or around the next bend in the road if you discard an idea or you are unwilling to turn a good idea into a great result.

Susan is passionate about focus and her commitment to your success is uncommon. Look into your crystal ball and imagine reaching the next level of success with a laser-like focus and new energy around meeting the best of what your clients need and want.

Every business owner would do well to use Susan's book as a light-house guide. And, if you have an opportunity to hear her speak or the privilege of working with her, you will never be the same. She will open your mind to a new way or thinking, acting and doing business. The game of business is worth playing. And, it is your turn.

Mark

Mark LeBlanc, CSP
Speaker
Author of *Never Be the Same, Growing Your Business and Build Your Consulting Practice*

INTRODUCTION

Isn't success great? If you're like me, having one success makes you highly motivated to create more successes. That was my feeling when I increased soup sales from 60% to 99% as a result of my soup experiment. It is how my many client companies feel once they've conducted successful experiments.

How do you create a series of successes?

Start with your strong fundamentals: your revenue, your offerings, your buyers. Look at them and allow yourself to imagine lots of 'what if' scenarios. These imaginings will generate hunches. Create experiments to test the best hunches. Use the Three-T model as your guide.

A sequence of small successes adds up to a whole that's greater than the sum of its part. The best thing about *Tinkering* is that you build on what you've already got. You can act quickly, the cost is low, and you build momentum.

THE CHANGE MYTH

You likely know Henry Ford's wise statement "If you always do what you've always done you'll get what you've always got." Yet there's a persistent myth that people fear and resist change. Where does that leave you, the business owner?

Did your company attract new buyers recently? Increase revenue? Hire a new employee or two? Broadcast a new marketing message? All of these actions are changes, yet you did them without hesitation because they helped you grow your company.

I strongly disagree with the idea that change is hard and people resist it. People do resist useless or meaningless change, so don't do change for change's sake.

Change in service to a clear and valuable outcome is not hard and people embrace it.

Tinker is about change. Change in small chunks and in service to a clear outcome.

I've written this book to show you that change isn't that hard. When undertaken in a thoughtful and creative way, change is a lot of fun. It improves company performance: revenue, profit, employee contributions, and customer and client engagement.

When you use the Three-T model, change becomes exhilarating and a habit.

THIS BOOK IS FOR YOU, THE BUSINESS OWNER

My most favorite people are owners who always want outcomes—exciting, big outcomes! They handle the inevitable problems with aplomb, and they meet their fundamental needs. It's into outcomes that they pour their passion and energy.

They want more. They want to turn their creative ideas into engines for true growth. And they want it soon, definitely sooner rather than later. They don't want to lose precious time trying to do it themselves. They represent the best of the small business sector that makes our economy sing.

Look inward for a moment. When you have an idea that could generate dramatic growth—but involves a bit of risk and some Singular Focus^{SM}—what's your gut response? Do you say "yes, let's get started" or do you say "I have to think about it."

I work with owners to actualize their plans, and my approach of choice is to *Tinker: How Smart Business Owners Develop Creative Ideas for True Growth.*

What you're about to read is a mindset and a model for embracing meaningful and valuable change.

TENETS, TECHNIQUES AND TACTICS

Before you dive into the Three-T Model, read my story about how a simple experiment with soup revolutionized my ability to successfully grow companies.

I've included worksheets and checklists that I use every day with my client companies. Writing things down is the most powerful tool for success. You record your experiments, measure results and variances, and keep track of your tinkering.

Remember, Thomas Edison built an entire laboratory in order to work on an electric light bulb. He recorded 10,000 ways that didn't work. He famously said "I didn't fail, I found 10,000 ways that don't work."

I want you to embrace the Three-T Model which includes Tenets of Trust, Techniques for Trying It and Tactics for Tinkering.

What powers me everyday is this: "There is no change unless I change."

The same holds true for you. Embrace it.

CHAPTER ONE
TRUE GROWTH

Many devoted business owners work hard and yet they never experience a "WOW!" moment, much less a "WOW!" year or period of years. I experienced this myself years ago and it bothered me until I figured out what was missing. Since then I have built my consulting practice on the idea that with certain specific efforts, all owners can create their own "WOW!" for years.

There is growth and then there is True Growth. Growth is the small revenue and profit increases a company experiences year over year, say 3-5%. These increases are enough to keep a company going, but not enough to help owners generate owner wealth and well being.

WHAT IS TRUE GROWTH?

There are many aspects to True Growth. Smart business owners embrace these and incorporate them regularly over years. A smart business owner knows he or she is never finished growing.

True growth is when a company understands positioning—the position of their company in the buyer's mind—and works to maintain or improve that position. It doesn't come from branding, discounts or occasional promotions.

True growth is when a company analyzes their financials for clues about how to increase top and bottom line growth. Who is buying what, and how often? Where are we experiencing changes and why? What do we do with what we have measured?

True growth is when a company looks for things that are repeatable; the same thing done again and again for the same product and service and/or the same buyer segment to increase frequency of repeat purchases (e.g. outbooking; "you bought these things together before, would you like to buy them together again?")

True growth is when a company looks for activities that are replicable; an activity or process that can be applied to different offerings and/or different buyers (such as my soup experiment applied to other lines)

True growth is when a company focuses on actions that have longevity, such as cultivating and nurturing their current buyers.

True growth is when a company focuses on innovations and improvements to current offerings.

True growth is when a company develops deep customer relationships

True growth is when a company infuses all employees with an understanding of how they contribute to revenue (e.g. teach everyone about your offerings so they see where their work fits in).

True growth is enjoyed by companies that cultivate and nurture their own employees and other stakeholders, such as vendors and suppliers.

True growth is when a company keeps its products and services limited enough so it can do amazing things with what it has, like innovations and improvements and extraordinary customer service.

True growth is when a company implements a C&N plan that they're really serious about. They target one segment that has great potential, rather than trying to be all things to all people.

True growth is earned through constructive and determined differentiation, not by following the latest fads or trends.

True growth is a culture of company-wide success shared by all with enthusiasm and sincerity.

A MINDSET AND A BEHAVIOR SET

True growth happens when the smart business owner focuses on making it happen. It's a mindset as well as a behavior set. It is all day, every day, month after month and year after year. It is also fun, exciting and very rewarding!

There is no change unless you change.

TRUE GROWTH CHECKLIST

Which True Growth practices already exist in your company?

What can you do to add them, or improve the ones you already have?

True Growth Practice	Yes or No?	Options for Action
Positioning your company to be Top of Mind for your buyers		
Analyzing financials for subtle clues to growth		
Repeatable practices that increase revenue		
Replicable processes applied to other segments		
Cultivating and Nurturing current buyers		

Improving and innovating current offerings to increase value		
Developing deep customer relationships		
Ensuring all employees understand how they contribute to revenue		
Cultivating and nurturing vendors and suppliers		
Delivering extraordinary customer service		
Aligning marketing with each customer segment		
Creating meaningful differentiation for buyers		
Establishing a company-wide culture of success that values all contributors		

CHAPTER TWO
THE UNIMAGINABLE

Never would I have imagined the dramatic changes to my life because of something as ordinary as soup.

Before then, it was extraordinary events that lead to dramatic changes in my life.

MAJOR UPHEAVAL

After 13 years of marriage, when I was just 39, my husband suffered a fatal heart attack in his sleep. Being a young widow is nothing you can prepare for. As I learned, grief takes its time. The path is uneven at best, and immobilizing at worst. For two years I struggled with sadness, anger and fear.

The sadness was the worst. The story of our relationship began like a fairytale. He was a widower with two young sons. He'd been dating a flashy woman everyone was bowled over by, even though she was wrong for him. She was a glamorous woman and while Bob may have been working in the fashion shoe business, he was happiest playing with his kids and reading sports box scores in his comfortable chair at home.

I invited him for dinner, and from that evening on, we were a couple. I embraced his little boys with fierce tenderness. I felt shivers of joy when, a few months after our wedding, one of the boys said "bye, *Mom*" for the first time.

Fairytales start sweet, turn rough and difficult, and then the characters live happily ever after. We had our very difficult times, but we'd started feeling things were on the upswing. On what would be our last night out together, we resolved an argument from earlier in the day, toasted with our beer mugs and began making plans for our next summer vacation.

Eight hours later, Bob was dead. The fairytale was over.

I was angry about the repercussions our difficulties had on my relationship with my step sons. They were my children. For reasons I never understood, Bob would say to me from time to time "I hope you love them like your own." He said it in front of them and of course, this sowed seeds of doubt. When times are tough, as they are after a sudden death, those doubts can grow into major barriers. Eventually the young men I called my sons broke off all contact with me.

I learned a lot about fear during this time. The worst was fear of the unknown. For years I'd pictured my life pretty much as it had been, married with kids, extended family, vacations, and other interests. With the marriage ended by Bob's death, and the kids leaving for their own lives, and temporary work that could cease at any time, the future was a big gray blank. Who was I now, I often wondered.

WITS AND GRIT

Other times, I've had to lean heavily on my wits and grit to get something I wanted that seemed out of reach.

I'll always remember my 13-year old self, at summer camp in Wisconsin. Our counselor told our cabin that we were to have the privilege of taking a three-day, off-camp trip. There were two choices: hiking or canoeing. Well, to me, 3 days of hiking, hot, dusty, dry, boring, was no privilege. So I would choose the canoe trip.

I faced a huge hurdle to that choice. I didn't have the swimming and canoeing skills required. I had always hated deep water and had never been in a canoe. In the space of three days, I dove into the deepest part of the lake and passed the swim test. I took a paddle class on the dock, then got in a canoe for the very first time and passed the canoeing test.

The canoe trip exceed my wildest dreams. That was the first time I was aware that I have wits and grit to overcome pretty steep challenges.

Many years later I faced a stark challenge: to get back on my beloved horse after a devastating fall, or give up Joey and the riding that I loved. I recognized that I needed some help learning to use, not disregard, my fear, so I spent a couple of months with a sports psychologist. I chose to commit to asking someone to hold Joey whenever I got on. My wits and my grit allowed me to continue riding for several more years.

EVERYDAY SOUP

It's no wonder then that dramatic changes wrought by soup, ordinary, everyday, soup, seemed so unimaginable.

Soup taught me many lessons, both for business and life.

I learned about **trust**: trust myself, trust others, trust processes, trust that the outcome will be illuminating even if you can't know what it is when you start.

I learned about **trying it**: try experiments, knowing some will fail miserably, some will be neutral and one or two rare ones will be extraordinary. Learning only happens from new experiences, from experiments that you create and implement with determination.

I learned about **tinkering**: nothing is ever perfect (ever!), and that is not the goal with tinkering. The goal of tinkering is improvement; creativity and innovation; and opening up what is unknown to you at the start. Tinkering leads back to trust, which leads again to trying it, which leads to more tinkering.

CHAPTER THREE
THE SOUP STORY

Whenever I speak to an audience of business owners, CEOs and partners, I tell them that my journey to be with them at that place and time started with soup. Yes, soup is the source of my passion for helping business owners make dramatic improvements in their companies and their lives.

In 1989 I moved away from the home I'd shared with my husband to a new city for a new job. I was to be the new, and first ever, executive director of a faith community. The Board of the community was quite excited to bring a fresh, new person to provide direction and innovation to their tired, old ways of doing things. Except that it turned out the whole board was not in favor, especially because it meant that the man who'd held the predecessor job was pushed into retirement before he was really ready.

The year was challenging, as I worked to incorporate the changes they expected from me tempered by the desire for things not to change too much. Primary among those who weren't too happy that I was there was the man who became the congregation's president when I'd been there about ten months. It didn't take long for him to become my harshest critic and make a case to the other Board members that I had to be relieved of my duties.

A few months later I was hired by another community and moved again. There I was faced with clergy who resented my efforts to manage a congregation that he had managed for decades. Eighteen months of turmoil later, again I was forced to leave.

One more time I put my hat in the ring for a position at another community, this time as Director of Development. This community was very kind and supportive as I dealt with my dying parents. Eventually though it was clear that the job and community were not a good fit for me, and I left.

At this point, I was floundering. I'd chosen to work in these communities because of the communities themselves. They were communities I wanted to belong to, not just jobs. But something wasn't working and I wasn't about to go through the emotional roller coaster again.

I decided that I would work for myself. I would find something to do that I could run the way I saw fit, and I'd take the risks and enjoy the rewards without hesitation.

I wandered around Northern Virginia for several months, looking at businesses of all kinds. In my mind I was trying on different industries and work to see what felt right. I became comfortable with the idea of opening a coffee shop or small food service business. This was in the 1994, when there were plenty of 'delis' that sold prewrapped sandwiches made of inexpensive deli meat and when coffee cafés were not on every corner. I thought I could do something special.

In those days, businesses for sale were advertised in the newspaper. I scoured the ads every day. One day, there it was! "Pastry shop for sale, Alexandria, VA." I called the broker, met him and the owner at the shop and pretty soon, I was the owner. I kept a big secret to myself: I had never even worked in a restaurant. But, hey, I loved to cook!

I named it Café Aurora, in honor of the goddess of the dawn. We would serve coffee, breakfast and lunch. I committed to this vision: Café Aurora serves restaurant quality food for carryout.

Anyone who's ever started a business knows how it completely takes over your life. This was the case with Café Aurora, and then some. I stood on my feet for hours every day, at first cooking along side the one cook I hired. We both served our customers and then ran over to the cash register to ring up the sale. I was able to hire another cook in a few months, and spend a bit more of my time getting to know our customers. We had a lively atmosphere and made every effort to engage with our customers, prepare quality food they loved and keep them coming back.

Slowly but surely Café Aurora began to hum. Each day began with eager coffee and breakfast seekers, and then we had a nicely busy lunch period. Keeping to my commitment to serve restaurant quality food for carryout, I changed the hot food menu frequently, kept the salad bar stocked with fresh items, and never served leftovers.

After one year I had the satisfaction of realizing that the Café was in the black. I was covering my payroll and all the bills, had many, many repeat customers and was making a bit of money myself.

No sooner had I sat back with satisfaction over this realization, than I had the urge to do more. I haven't ever been a "don't rock the boat" kind of person, and I was ready to shake things up.

SHAKING THINGS UP

"But what?" I wondered. Each day I'd look around the space—it was so small all of it was visible from any spot—and wonder what could I do next.

One day my eye fell on the counter where we placed our crocks of soup. We made three fresh soups every day and always discarded what didn't sell. As I looked at the crocks, I suddenly had a hunch! I thought I could do an experiment and make a difference in the amount of soup we sold.

Our typical approach to our menu was to look at the food we had in the refrigerator, freezer and on the shelves, and make a new menu each day. This was especially true with the soup. We had three categories of soup types: bean soups, broth soups and cream soups. Each day we'd make soups from our ingredients on hand, and the assortment of soup types would be totally random. Typically, all year long, we sold about 60% of each soup each day.

My hunch was that I could figure out how to sell more soup. I designed an experiment to test that hunch.

During the experiment, instead of random soups each day, we would sell only one type of soup every day for a week. Three different cream soups each day for a week; three different broth soups each day the following week; and three different bean soups each day the third week. I would keep detailed daily records of which soups we made and how much of each we sold.

I also told my cooks not to bring the experiment to the attention of our customers because I wanted really raw data. They would buy what they liked or not. I might lose a little soup revenue if someone didn't like the category of the week, but that would be worth it in the long run for the outcome I was after.

We began the experiment. Each day I'd record on a spreadsheet the soups of the day and at the end of the day I'd carefully measure and record what was left before discarding the leftovers.

At the end of three weeks I had a spreadsheet full of data. This was still when wide paper spreadsheets were common. I poured over my data to learn from their own behavior what our customers liked and what they didn't like. It was fascinating to get this glimpse into people's tastes. I had a vague idea before the experiment, from customer comments and from days when there was more or less soup left. Now I had proof!

My goal was to design the perfect soup menu. No more random soup selections. After studying the data, I wrote a soup menu for the coming week. Each day we would serve one best seller from each soup category. I did not know what would happen but I was really excited to begin on Monday.

My cooks made the chosen soups on Monday, one best selling cream, one best selling broth and one best selling bean. We placed the crocks on the soup counter as usual.

The day was busy and there was no time to check on the soups. At three o'clock we turned the lock on the door and ran over to the soup counter. Each of us put a hand on a lid, and in one motion we lifted the lids. There was no soup left in any of the crocks!

I tried to take it in stride. After all, it was only the first day. Could we repeat the sell out again on Tuesday?

We made the planned best seller soups for Tuesday and again at three o'clock we lifted the lids. All the soup was gone.

From that day on, until the day three years later when I sold the Café, we sold 100% of our soups almost every single day, year in and year out.

THE EXPERIMENT ALWAYS TEACHES A LESSON

After this success with soup I tried to do similar experiments with other products lines. I learned that successfully growing product lines requires three factors:

- Limited scope
- Willingness to take risks
- Importance of raw customer data

LIMITED SCOPE

We tried a similar experiment with our salad bar and it didn't work. That's when I learned the critical importance of limited scope. We always offered only three soups per day. We could accurately measure how much we started with and how much we had left. People accepted that the supply of soup might be less the later they came in for lunch.

We had about 25 items on our salad bar. Our customers expected that there would always be some supply left, even late into the lunch hour, so we refilled containers throughout the day. Thus we could never measure what we put out and what was left. It was impossible to keep track of refills during the busy lunch period.

When we tried similar experiments with segments of our hot menu, it helped a lot. For example, we did similar experiments with pasta dishes and with what we called American comfort foods. We were able to have more clarity about why we sold more of some dishes than others, even though to us they seemed similar.

And we did the same with desserts. All chocolate one week, no chocolate the next week, keeping track of sales and what was left. We reduced dessert waste by 38% after that experiment.

WILLINGNESS TO TAKE RISKS

During the three weeks of the soup experiment, I was aware that some soup customers chose not to buy any soup because they don't like one type of soup. The loss was probably 5%, which was well worth it given that we knew it was of limited duration.

We could not have learned as much as we did about soup preferences if we hadn't been willing to take this risk. I have always been a willing risk taker and the soup experiment confirmed that taking some risk always generates a solid return.

IMPORTANCE OF RAW CUSTOMER DATA

We made the deliberate choice to not tell our customers that we were conducting an experiment. We were curious to see what they did without any influence one way or the other. They could buy soup or not.

This was a bit of a change for us as we were in the habit of asking our customers what food they liked, and did not like, in order to serve them better. But those were informal conversations that could easily be skewed by their and our desire to be 'nice.'

Since those years, as a customer myself, I have been asked millions of time for my feedback via a survey or questionnaire. It's often clear that the survey writer is trying to get certain answers. The soup experiment did not do that, and I believe that's why we had such amazing success with soup for years afterwards.

When I was ready to exit Café Aurora, prospective buyers liked our P & L. I attribute the solid financials to the soup experiment and to successfully applying the lessons learned for the remaining time I owned the Café.

TRUST, TRY, TINKER

Since Café Aurora, I have applied the lessons learned from the soup experiment to hundreds of other businesses. Most important is that as the world has changed (in 1994 when I bought the café there was no internet as we know it today, and email was a strange new thing) I've adapted the lessons to changing times.

Trust, Try and Tinker remain hugely valuable. In the rest of this book you will learn how to apply them to your current business.

Trust my gut, my instinct, myself. I know the business, I know human behavior, I am creative and innovative.

Try it. Create experiments. Some will be simple, like the soup, others will be complicated. Some will feel really risky. Do them anyway. It will be worth it for what you learn.

Tinker with it. Use what you learn from your trust and your experiment and improve. Maybe you discard and start over. Maybe one success leads to another one.

Tinkering is how smart business owners develop creative ideas for true growth.

THE THREE-T MODEL: TRUST, TRY, TINKER

In the beginning I just had hunches, I did experiments and I tinkered until I felt the best results had been achieved.

After helping various business owners with one of the Ts or another, I realized my clients would reach maximum results if I created a system as an example to follow or imitate.

The Three-T Model was born.

Models tell you that a sequence of activities, combined with certain elements, will produce an outcome.

The outcome is a measurable change in the current situation. For each application of the Three-T Model, you choose a specific outcome.

The sequence of activities are Trust yourself, Try experiments, and Tinker with them for better results.

The elements include: your business, your expertise, your instinct and hunches, your customers and offerings, and some boundaries.

I want you to picture yourself using the model for your own company. Understand the Tenets of Trust, practice the Techniques for Trying It; and enthusiastically embrace the Tactics for Tinkering.

3-T MODEL

TRUST	TRY	TINKER
Hunch	**Experiment**	**Analyze**
Bubbles up from your knowledge and experience	Limit scope	**Decide**
	Some risk	**Implement**
	Capture raw data	**Tinker**
		One dimension at a time
		One week at a time
		Yes/No
		Repeat with another dimension

CHAPTER FOUR
TRUST

Hunches are not accidents. They are hard earned, the result of years of work and lessons learned. They don't come from out of the blue, they bubble up from a place of knowledge and expertise within. Embrace your hunches; take action.

I'll always remember the hot summer day when I met Jerry, the CPA. He had just authorized his payroll and was feeling the sting of an ever-decreasing bank balance. Mid-summer was the worst month for his firm because it was so heavily reliant on revenue from tax return services. The drought begins every year in May and lasts until September.

I had a hunch that Jerry could generate much more revenue during these summer months, which was what I was there to talk with him about. I explained my ideas and he was skeptical. My hunch required a major mindset shift—his mind!—and he was really hesitant.

He finally agreed to conduct an experiment. We would start small, and if the experiment didn't work, he would be relatively unscathed.

Five weeks later he called to tell me that the experiment was a huge success! His clients loved what he did and many were eager to sign up for his new offerings.

My hunch for Jerry came from my years of experience with buyers: buyers love to be paid attention to and feel important to the company's owner. The only question for any owner is what specific attention will convey that they are important. In Jerry's case the experiment was simple, elegant and it worked.

Trust is critical to creating true growth; to making progress and achieving bigger and more dramatic results.

We have to trust ourselves—our hunches, our decisions, our actions and our commitment. And we have to trust others.

When I bought the pastry shop that I turned into Café Aurora, I trusted that I could learn to run a food service business, even though I had no experience whatsoever! I trusted that I could hire some good people, and that I could create an atmosphere that would be enjoyable for customers.

I had no proof of any of these things. I did have a history of approaching challenges with wits and grit. That was really the basis of my trust.

That trust in myself was well-placed.

Learn these Tenets of Trust.

1. Go with your instinct or your gut. You've been around long enough to have plenty of lessons learned. They are giving you your hunches, ideas or gut feelings. Accept them as valid.

2. Do not listen to that negative voice in your head. It's the one telling you not to trust yourself. That voice will sneeringly say "Hah, you don't know anything about that." Or it will sound like a bully "Nah, nah, you can't do anything right, you clumsy, stupid thing." You know that voice. Remember this: you do not have to listen to it.

3. Develop your hunches into actionable ideas. Start with the desired outcome (sell more soup; generate revenue during the normally slow period). What are 2 or 3 high level steps needed to start on the path to the outcome?

4. Share your hunch with only a small number of trusted people. Be clear that you are sharing to inform them, and that you aren't seeking their approval. No one but you gets to decide to listen to, and act on, a hunch.

5. Write a detailed plan with dates/times; person/people responsible; discrete action steps; data collection. You won't know everything you'll encounter so write what you do know and be prepared to course correct when needed. Flexibility is a virtue.

6. Be generous to yourself. Things may not go as you planned; you may feel stupid or perplexed. Stop thinking like that. That's the whole point of hunches—they are not guaranteed, but without them you are stuck.

It's sometimes difficult to trust ideas, especially when they push you out of your habitual thinking. I often have a strong hunch for a client and face the client's own discomfort with that hunch. I work hard to get the client to adopt the idea behind the hunch.

"You mean I have to make the calls myself?" Jerry had asked me when we were discussing my hunch. I had suggested he invite about 25 clients to an informal after-hours event where he'd serve refreshments and have someone speak about of topic of interest to high net worth individuals.

The hunch was that **personal outreach** that reinforced the closeness of his relationship with clients would help them see Jerry as a much more valuable resource, way beyond his tax expertise. An email invite would be a useful follow-up, but the initial invitation had to be via a phone call from him. He had been hoping his office manager could make the calls.

I insisted that he had to make the calls. He started on the guest list and suddenly had an epiphany: his clients, most of whom he had known for a decade or longer, were thrilled to get his call. The personal touch meant more than anything.

Whether it's my own hunch or the hunch or gut instinct of a client, I find tremendous value in trusting the hunch. To have a hunch means you have something inside you that's coming to the surface and showing you a way forward.

Remember, hunches aren't random. Embrace your hunches.

CHAPTER FIVE
TRY IT

HOW TO TRY IT

In thinking about trying it, I'm reminded of the owner of an independent auto services company. He was used to being the point person for all customer inquiries. He did this out of necessity when he first opened the business and had only one technician. Now, twenty+ years later, it was his habit and his security blanket. He didn't want to try turning that role over to someone else.

As he and I worked to implement several revenue growing techniques, we kept coming back to this part of his role. He had a service writer at the front counter who was capable of taking names, phone numbers and brief descriptions of service needs, but nothing more. All his customers talked to the owner for every choice or decision.

His goal, the one that had motivated him to work with me, was to reduce the time he spent on the premises. In order to make that possible he had to have a well-trained and knowledgeable— and yes, a higher paid—person at the front desk. But he didn't want to try it. He worried, just like so many people do, that it wouldn't work—that this change would fail.

As he embraced and succeeded with other initiatives I helped him implement, he began to weigh more thoughtfully having a new, better person in that front desk role. After much anguished deliberation, he agreed to try it, and we set about finding the right person. We interviewed many, and finally there was the perfect candidate. He was a disabled vet who had worked with military vehicles for years. He was having a hard time finding a job and wanted this one very much.

Within two months, the owner called to tell me that he hardly spoke to customers anymore. His front desk guy was doing it all and the customers loved him.

TECHNIQUES FOR TRYING

1. The most important technique for trying is to set a start date and stick to it. Remember that how you use your time reflects your priorities. If something is worth trying, it is worth setting a firm date and taking action on that date.

2. Delineate clear boundaries for things you're going to try. Saying you're going to 'try marketing better' is vague

and amorphous. Saying you're going to try cultivating and nurturing your best buyers with a one year C&N plan creates perfect boundaries. You know what's in and what's not in.

3. Make the effort a manageable size. Saying you're going to 'try social media' is way too big. Instead say you're going to try LinkedIn by getting a half day of coaching from a LinkedIn expert.

4. Give yourself time to get comfortable with whatever you're trying. Everything gets better with time. The first day the new service writer started work for my auto services client, everyone was understandably nervous and a bit tense. After three days things were better, and after three weeks, it was clear that he was a success.

5. Keep good records of what you're trying. How do you start, what resources do you use, who else is involved? How long will the experiment last? Keep records as the experiment generates data. Excellent records are key to making use of the experiment results for the long term.

6. Have a clear end date of the experiment. This is the date at which you review or analyze your data; draw some conclusions; and decide to keep going, to stop, or to make changes suggested by your analysis.

7. Share your results with your executives, employees, trusted advisors, family members and professionals that support your business. Trying new things—experiments—is a sign of a vibrant, growing business with

a creative owner at its head. No matter what the final analysis—or especially if you conclude that the experiment was a bust—sharing the results sends the message that you're never satisfied with the status quo.

CHANGE HOW YOU THINK ABOUT FAILURE

My most profound insight came from thinking about **how to think about failure**. I realized that when I, or any client, says "I tried this and I failed" we are shortchanging ourselves. The full statement should be "I tried X and I failed to achieve the outcome Y that I was aiming for." The difference is that you can then go on to say: "I learned a lot more about X than I ever knew before. I also have some ideas about how to do X better, or to do Z instead."

A lawyer was about 18 months into her own law firm when we spoke. She was trying to grow and kept running into a solid brick wall: her own perfectionism. She said "I am failing at being perfect in a short period of time." She acknowledged that perfectionism takes time, and the more she spends on perfecting things, the fewer things she has time for.

I suggested that she evaluate every task on a continuum from zero (0) "nothing bad will happen" to ten (10) "it's a matter of life and death." Each letter, article, filing, blog post, speech and phone call would fall someplace on the continuum. She would need some lines of demarcation on the continuum. From 0 to 4, nothing bad would happen and she could get the work done quickly and let it go. From 5-7, she would spend more time, and from 8-10, she would seek to be perfect.

A few months later she let me know that this had helped her tremendously: she was making more money and had more free time for a second, non-law related, business. Her exact words were: "Susan, I am so glad I tried the continuum approach. It made a world of difference."

You'll Never Know Until You Try

CHAPTER SIX
TINKER

Tinkering is the commitment to making adjustments to the experiments, or to your normal ways of doing things, that generally seem to be working. You tinker when you think there may be **untapped opportunities**.

The General Manger of an HVAC company hired me to help them increase revenue from homeowners. I always begin by focusing on current buyers, increasing repeat purchases and then new purchases.

The GM had instituted a script for customer service reps (CSRs) a few years earlier in response to chaos. While the script tamed the chaos, it didn't seem to be helping increase revenue or endearing customers to the company. The most common customer review online was a 3—average—for customer satisfaction. Customers often commented that CSRs seemed disinterested or unhelpful.

I listened to several dozen calls. In short order it was clear that the script did not reflect the reality of these employees' calls with customers.

I recommended to the General Manager that we tinker with the script. He would first clearly articulate the company's values: honesty, reliability, accuracy. Then we would embed those values into the script, replacing speed and consistency of responses. He was nervous but agreed. We ended up tinkering for three weeks, each week with some variations that we evaluated and kept or discarded. By the end of the tinkering, the CSRs were much more responsive to the actual things callers said, and revenue and reviews were on the upswing.

OPPORTUNITIES FOR TINKERING

Marketing: Many companies tinker with their marketing, making small changes to designs or messages in collateral that is generally working. One of the best known tinkering approaches is A/B testing, where only small, controlled elements are changed and distributed to similar audiences. You measure which format generates the best results.

Customer segmentation: Other times companies tinker with their customer segmentation. Many times companies don't segment at all, so the initial effort at segmenting falls into the "Try It" category. After trying it for awhile, the company begins tinkering, making specific, targeted changes and measuring results.

Products and Services: I've also worked with business owners on their line of products and services. Often the first step is a big "Try It" moment. They launch a new product or service based on customer feedback. After a specific time period, they begin tinkering with the new offering, in terms of size, duration, price, and most importantly, value. A company can often add significant value their buyers will pay for, without a significant increase in their costs.

Internal communications: You can tinker with internal communications. Some companies find shared online calendars work well. Other companies think shared calendars disrupt individual's work. Instead of going all in or not at all, tinker with an online calendar tool that gives your company the results you need.

External communications: You can tinker with communications out to your customers and clients. I always endorse trying new communication tools and after a decent period of experimentation, evaluating and tinkering. Look at frequency; content; length; audience; design; platform. Tinker with one element at a time so you get clear measures of how the change is working. If you like something, tinker with another thing, keeping all else steady. And so on.

Other external communications go to partners, vendors, competitors, and perhaps media, industry forums and others. Experiment with each of these as appropriate. Tinker with them one at a time. Keep what works, discard what doesn't and move on.

Sales: There are many opportunities to tinker with your sales approach. First, ask how your current sales process, or funnel, is working. Begin tinkering with areas or elements that are getting mediocre results. Maybe you have a consistently good attraction phase but your qualifying phase isn't great. You either qualify too many or don't qualify enough. Tinker just with the qualifying phase for three weeks. Then make adjustments and move to the next phase that could be working better.

Financials: Most company Owners study their P&L each month. They look at the top line and the bottom line and think "we're doing well" or "we're doing poorly." Instead, tinker with your approach to viewing and understanding your P&L. For example, break out one product line and look at it for the past 12 months. What's the revenue pattern? What is the cost pattern? And the profit pattern? What opportunities for tinkering with that product line are possible? This is so much more effective than a company wide overhaul which will never pinpoint what changes truly made the difference.

TACTICS FOR TINKERING

These are the most effective tactics for tinkering. Apply one or apply them all—but TINKER!

1. Break multi-step processes or approaches into chunks. Select small and clearly defined targets for tinkering.

2. Do not feel bound to tinker in order or sequence. Look for the highest value opportunities for tinkering and focus on them.

3. Document the current situation: use metrics or a narrative to describe the current state.

4. Set a limited time frame for the tinkering, such as one, two or three weeks. Usually three weeks is ideal but if you're careful, you can learn a lot in less time.

5. Keep detailed records of your tinkering actions.

6. After completing your tinkering, use the data you've collected to decide to make the end point permanent; or decide to revert to a prior condition. It is critically important that you make a definite decision. Do not leave the results on the shelf someplace "for later." You will lose momentum and worse, lose credibility with everyone who participated in the tinkering.

You must return to TRUST. Trust that you've done enough to make it work; that your hunches came from your experiences; and that you can always tinker again.

OPPORTUNITIES FOR TINKERING

Tinkering Type	Start date	Actions	End date	Outcomes
Fees Improve Price-to-Value Ratio				
Customer Service More Personalized				
Out-booking				
Innovate Best Selling Product				

Tinkering Type	Start date	Actions	End date	Outcomes
Other?				

CHAPTER SEVEN
THE MOMENT MY TINKERING PAID OFF BIG

When I established Trivers Consulting Group, one key decision I had to make was how to get paid for my work. Everyone I talked to said "charge by the hour." When I asked how I figured out my hourly rate they said: "Figure out how much money you need to make per week and divide that by 40. That's your hourly rate."

I didn't question this because *everyone* was doing it.

A few years later one wise person posed this question to a group of consultants: "If your client is better off getting their results sooner rather than later, and you're better off working more hours and delivering results later, doesn't charging by the hour create an ethical conflict with your client?"

Dead silence. Then it dawned on us. Yes, this was an ethical conflict.

The longer I continued to charge by the hour the more this conflict weighed on me. I wasn't delaying or dragging out my work intentionally, but could the time/revenue relationship that dwelled in the back of my mind cause me to go slow?

Other issues about hourly billing began to nag me. This practice actually gave clients permission to use me for fewer hours than they really needed because they were so cost conscious. If that meant the project delivered less, they would associate their disappointment with my work, not with their deliberate cost reduction management.

Clients were often worried about the total cost so they'd look for the lowest hourly rate rather than the best qualified. If they couldn't really control the final cost, at least they could control the rate that created the final bill.

Clients would question me about me how I was spending the time I was billing them for. Did I charge for travel time? How much? Why not half the actual number of hours? Why pay for any travel time at all?

Did it count when I spent time answering emails or reading documents at home and sending in my comments and recommendations? What proof did I have that I spent as much time doing these things as I billed them for?

Another issue was unexpected delays or problems. Should I bill them for work that had to be redone or even discarded? When they were paying for my time, that certainly seemed 'fair' yet it was infuriating and caused a lot of friction.

In sum, I began to see hourly billing as destructive to the relationships I worked hard to establish and nurture, and to the final outcome of the work.

When I tried to share my discomfort with others, they'd immediately argue two points: 1) hourly rates ensured that if the work ballooned out of control, they'd at least get paid for all of it; and 2) when the work is complex, you can never know the full extent of a project at the beginning. Their argument was that the client, not the consultant, should assume the risk.

Because of the ethical conflict and the risk to the client, I put my mind to searching for a solution. My hunch was that there could be a way to remove these two issues. Hourly billing and the justifications for it were focused on inputs—or really one input only, time.

The answers began to develop when I formulated the question this way: "What if I looked at outcomes instead of inputs?"

Several iterations later, I knew the question I needed to answer:

"How can I provide tremendous value to clients and earn a fee related to the value the client receives?"

I looked back at several client projects from the past 12 months. I experimented in my mind with conversations with those clients. What would I have said that would make a fee related to their outcome make sense—or even make them happy? How would I demonstrate that they were better off if we thought of our work as leading to an outcome, rather than as an accumulation of the input of time?

I tried out a few of my ideas with some other independent professionals. Not one agreed with me! The conversations always went back to their own perceived risk. They'd feared they would underprice and overwork.

Next I tried out my ideas with people who hire people for their expertise; people similar to my clients. Some of them objected immediately on the grounds that they couldn't be sure they were getting what they paid for. They felt that paying for hours of time was concrete. Even if they had no discernible value from the time they paid for.

I did find a few people who listened and engaged in a conversation with me. They were curious what I meant by outcomes. They wanted examples, and they wanted to understand how to assess that the outcome was received. These were great conversations that helped me tinker with my idea of providing my services for a fee that represented the value to the client.

While I was going through this process of trusting my hunch, trying ideas and tinkering with them, I continued to offer my services on an hourly basis, even as the ethical conflict and the risk issue plagued me. Then one day I was ready. I typed up a memo to myself and posted it in my sight line above my desk:

From now on I will only offer my services for a fixed fee commensurate with the value to the client.

Not an hour later a man called. He'd been referred to me and was interested in having me work with a team that was competing for an enormous contract.

During our conversation it was clear that we would be a great fit to do this work. As is typical of these conversations, he eventually asked what it could cost. I looked at my memo, took a deep breath and said "I'd love to work with your team. I do my work for a fixed fee based on the outcome we're going to work towards. If you give me 24 hours I'll have a proposal for you." As my heart pounded and I barely breathed, he said "That would be great!" And that was the first time I implemented my value-based fee approach and I have never looked back.

Tinkering is how smart business owners develop creative ideas for true growth. What's your idea and how are you going to tinker with it?

CHAPTER EIGHT
IT'S YOUR TURN

"Someday" is not a day of the week, nor can you find it on any calendar. This means that anything you promise to do someday will not get done. You'll continue to do what you've always done, and the outcomes you envision as the keys to your owner wealth and well being will never happen.

The beauty of T*inkering: How Smart Business Owners Develop Creative Ideas for True Growth* is that you can start today. You can start today because you only need one small outcome in mind. Let your mind wander until a hunch about how you could achieve that outcome bubbles up. Design a simple experiment and begin implementing it. In three weeks' time you'll have raw data that you can analyze. Then make a decision and go.

And so on, as you pursue other outcomes that add up to True Growth over the next 6-12 months.

I hope you've read each chapter of this book and developed an overall understanding of what it means to Tinker. To help you actually get started today, here's a summary of the action steps. Pick an outcome and get started.

You are in control: there is no change unless you change.

You need these ingredients for a successful Tinker:

- Limit the scope
- Take some risk
- Collect raw data

TRUST

What do you often think about? Whatever it is, it is the most fertile environment for a hunch to bubble up.

- Are you zealous about your customer service?
- Eager to see revenue numbers rise?
- Have lots of ideas about improving or innovating your current products or services?
- Think a lot about your bottom line?
- Worried a lot about competition?

Hunches don't come out of nowhere. They bubble up from your experience, knowledge and quests for improvements.

One of my favorite techniques for creating the mental openness for hunches to bubble up is walking. I walk alone or with my dog and without electronics. I actually ask myself "what will I think about during this walk?" Then I accept whatever answer arises and I actively think about it.

- What do I know about this topic?
- Why would this topic have come up now?
- What would it mean if I did something about it?
- What could that something be?

And so on. When I return to the office I write down my ideas or questions.

Most important is that I schedule time the next day for working on that idea. One hour, at my desk, to figure out if there is something there I want to focus on. Can I describe an outcome I'd like to achieve?

I also make a quick calculation about the extent of risk in the idea. It's important to know how much risk there is. Why? Because low risk efforts are often not worth it and because higher risk efforts have the potential to be worth a lot. I like a simple scale or continuum. Zero is no risk and 10 is a lot of risk. Where between zero and 10 does this outcome fall? I know that the higher the risk, the higher the potential return. But potential is key, so I want to judge that first. If the idea I'm thinking about falls between 6 and 9, I'll usually pursue it. Ideas that falls at 5 or below do not have enough return for me to spend any effort on.

TRY IT

Once you've had a hunch, you have to design an experiment to test the hunch. The experiment phase of Tinkering provides two benefits: 1) it is small enough in scale that it doesn't consume everything in sight and 2) it lets you know what could happen if you do adopt it permanently.

To make trying it worthwhile you have to commit enough time and attention to the experiment.

What is *enough* time and attention?

My guideline is 3 hours to set up the experiment. I like 3 hours because it feels generous but not wasteful. You don't have to rush and you know there is a start and an end time.

Critical to a successful experiment is saying "no" to anything that will interfere with this set up time. No calls, no emails, no visitors at your door. NO distractions. Be prepared for this to be hard the first time. People used to interrupting you will be flummoxed that you won't let them, and your own busy mind will wonder what you're missing. Be strong, it gets easier!

Your experiment has to be specific. What are you doing to create the experiment? What will you measure? How will you measure it? How will you record your measurements? When will it start and when will it end? Build in a couple of interim milestones, such as a certain number of days or a certain number of participants.

Keep records. Don't analyze them or worry them to death during the experiment. That tempts you to make changes midstream, which then distorts the data.

At the end of the experiment, gather all your data and set aside time to analyze it and think. Another 3 hours here would be great.

TINKER

Once you've completed the experiment and analyzed the data, you have to make one or more decisions. Do not put this off. You have momentum going for you and your mind is fully engaged. You're best situated for a terrific outcome at this very moment.

Your decision is about what to do now that you have your data.

- Do you make a change or changes?
- What are they?
- Who needs to be involved?
- Are there any costs?
- What goals will you set?
- How will you track the impact of the changes?

This is an exciting opportunity for your company to get a boost. Keep in mind, a series of modest wins adds up to big gains over time.

Once you've decided in favor of a change, you begin to track the results. This is when tinkering can begin. It takes about 60 days to know how the change is impacting the company. Once you see the impacts you can think about, and begin, tinkering.

Let me be really clear here: there are times when something is working just wonderfully. Halt any further tinkering. Those are times to celebrate. And they leave you free to turn your attention to the next hunch and experiment.

It's your turn! What's your hunch, your experiment and your outcome?

• • • • • • • • •

Read the Case Studies on the next pages. You'll see how owners like yourself have let hunches bubble up, designed experiments to test them, and made decisions following their analysis of the data. Some tinkered to make a good idea even better.

All companies are better off today than they were before their experiments and the owners are happier than ever.

SUCCESS STORIES
HOW TINKERING HELPED SMART BUSINESS OWNERS DEVELOP CREATIVE IDEAS FOR TRUE GROWTH

CUSTOMER SERVICE

When customers and clients have problems they want answers right away. No matter how chill a person might be under normal circumstances, when times are not normal, chill is replaced by anxiety and tension. The home remodel company I worked with found this to cause extreme stress on its employees and negative impacts on their reputation.

The co-owners wanted my help reducing the anxiety and tension, in order to improve their relationships and create opportunities for additional work.

During our discovery, the co-owners told me they keep their staff count low in order to minimize costs. The effect of this was that no one in the company was assigned to respond imme- diately to customer calls of any type. Customers had to leave a message and someone would get back to them "as soon as possi- ble." When the call was about a problem encountered during a remodel project, "as soon as possible" was a bad response.

My hunch was that a dedicated customer relationship manager could make a huge difference in two ways. First, it would im- prove the experience on both sides of the remodel project and second, it would help the homeowners return to this same com- pany for future remodeling projects.

The co-owners objected on the basis of cost. They saw this role as purely a cost that reduced profits.

In this case the experiment to test this hunch was to do a ret- rospective of the remodeling projects they did for the past 18 months. We would look at the initial plans including the rev- enue, costs and the timeline, and compare them to the actual cost and timeline. We would read all the notes the project man- ager kept, and highlight anything that indicated problems. We would determine how long it took to address the problem and the costs associated with it.

The result was that the total costs to the company of the delays and remediation of mistakes wasn't that high—but it was more than the total compensation package of a dedicated customer relationship manager.

Additionally, we estimated what additional remodeling proj- ects these clients might want if they were really happy with the company's work and responsiveness on the first project. Even a conservative estimate made it clear that the cost of a customer relationship manager was easily covered and then some.

Several months later they shared with me an enthusiastic note they received from a homeowner. The note emphasized how the homeowner appreciated the customer relationship manager making the project so enjoyable even though there were a couple of hiccups.

CLIENT RELATIONSHIPS

Certain companies typically provide services only one time to their clients. I call these one-and-done buyers. Companies include but aren't limited to, architects, personal injury lawyers, builders, M&A firms, some medical specialists, and suppliers related to these companies

Every owner of these companies wonders why should they cultivate and nurture these one-and-done buyers? And if there is a good reason, how would they do it?

Two of my client companies have learned why and how. Here are their stories.

PERSONAL INJURY LAW FIRM

This firm comprises two lawyers who have been very successful since they launched their law firm about a half dozen years ago. They have won large awards for their clients and have innumerable testimonials to their kindness and caring as well as their legal acumen. I began working with the partners to help them attract cases that would not be subject to any state-imposed award caps.

They hope that their clients will not suffer subsequent personal injuries, so marketing to those clients for additional business is unrealistic, not to mention in poor taste. What kind of cultivate and nurture plan could we create that would let people know the kinds of cases they are looking for?

I had a hunch that the relatives of their clients would welcome some ongoing personal touches from the lawyers. Every personal injury case involves family and close friends as well as the injured person. We designed a two-part experiment. The first part was a nice hand-signed note from the partners to all family members of previous clients, that recognized their support to the injured person and how that helped during the long months of the case and trial. A few weeks later, the partners called each of the family members to ask for their feedback now that the case was over. Included in the questions were a couple about what other information the family or friend would appreciate having. Options included medical support resources and financial planning resources. The partners had established relationships with some caregivers and wealth managers that they felt entirely secure in recommending.

The response to the experiment was terrific. About 95% of the family and friends were so grateful for being recognized and for the recommendations. Following the experiment we decided to tinker a bit with the questions and the recommendations. We also decided they would implement the two part plan within 6-8 weeks of the end of every case going forward.

The long term follow up includes articles and recommended resources to the family sent 6 times per year. They offer no-fee short consultations if future problems arise.

One year after the start of this Cultivate and Nurture plan, the firm has received more than a dozen referrals from family and friends of their clients.

THE ARCHITECT

I was introduced to the architect by a friend of his. This friend, and the architect's wife, were concerned that he hadn't adopted the typical tools of modern architecture, namely CAD technology for drawing plans and social media for marketing and promotion. They thought I could talk some sense into him.

He immediately told me that he doesn't want to use technology to grow his business. When he described how he draws by hand, and in pencil, every line of a home or large remodel three times at least, I had a hunch he had something unique upon which to build his business. His goal was one additional project per year.

He told me that he gets almost all his new clients through referrals from previous clients. Word of mouth is pretty customary in the circles his clients are immersed in.

The experiment we created was a simple client satisfaction survey. They key to its success was that he would call each of his clients from the past three years and talk over the survey with them. It was designed to elicit conversation, not just answers. All the questions were open-ended, high-gain questions.

Of the 17 clients he called, 16 of them were still in their homes, enjoying every minute there. Their answers were about happy events and included meaningful reflections. Almost every one mentioned how much they had enjoyed the process of working with him as he hand-drew their plans.

From this raw data, we created a new, strong mission and vision for his company. His mission is to create living spaces that meet all the needs—physical, financial and emotional--of his clients. His vision is that every client appreciates and values his beautiful, hand-drawn designs and plans.

We designed a Cultivate and Nurture plan that keeps these clients up to date on the latest architectural and housing news and trends. He also asked two of them if he could host an appreciation event at their homes. He would make and finance all the arrangements. He wanted them to invite their friends and neighbors, and he would be there to speak and answer questions. He made a special gift for the two host families: gorgeous hand-drawn pictures of their homes, beautifully framed. There were gasps of admiration from the guests when these were unveiled.

Those two events, held about 4 months apart, generated more serious inquiries than he had ever received in one year. He now proudly and consistently draws his plans by hand and doesn't give much thought to social media.

PRODUCT DEVELOPMENT

The organizational development consulting firm principal was frustrated. They had been trying to grow the firm for close to two years. Revenue wasn't as steady as he wanted and he didn't really know what was missing. We agreed to work together for six months with the goal of increasing revenue.

During our initial discovery, the principal told me that his firm was primarily known for its ability to help companies improve employee morale following a disruption of some kind. The executives of struggling firms would call his company to repair the immediate situation and overcome whatever problems were handcuffing them. Once the morale situation was repaired, the engagement ended.

My client knew that his clients would be better off if they learned how to build and sustain employee morale under a variety of circumstances. Organizations continually face difficult situations and it's much better to prepare for them than to recover from them.

The firm offered a variety of programs to help build and sustain employee morale no matter what happens.

I had a hunch that most people familiar with the firm didn't really know the full range of value the firm offered. We designed an experiment to test that hunch.

The experiment was to call 50 people in a period of three weeks and ask one question. These were people who know the company. The principal introduced himself and said "We're trying to clarify our message, may I ask you a question?" He then asked "If someone asked you what do you know about our company, what would you say?" He would not discuss the response or react, just record the answer, say thanks, and end the call.

He got answers from 45. It turned out that everyone said they "fix employee morale." Almost no one said they offered programs that would prevent morale problems. That told us what we needed to know.

You can't create demand for morale repair, but you can create demand for building sustainable employee morale under many difficult situations.

The outcome of the experiment was to create two distinct marketing tracts: 1) a campaign to market their "create a healthy organization" offerings and 2) one to ensure that the firm was top of mind when morale repair was needed.

After the first round of marketing efforts, we analyzed responses and tinkered a bit with the message and the recipients. The firm is now receiving more calls about getting their expertise to create a healthy organization.

ABOUT THE AUTHOR

Susan Trivers founded Trivers Consulting Group in 2000. Since then she has worked with hundreds of companies, helping them capitalize on their current buyers, current offerings and current employees. Her Vision: Every business owner builds value and wealth as soon as possible and for as long as possible. Her values: honesty, integrity, high value.

Susan's consulting is the outgrowth of her philosophy of **Singular Focus**SM. Executives develop an extreme degree of focus on driving revenue. The response has been overwhelmingly positive. The business enjoys dramatic revenue growth with more profits flowing to the bottom line.

Susan Trivers was previously the owner of Café Aurora in Alexandria, VA. It was there that she had a hunch, did an experiment and created astonishing results. This book, *Tinkering: How Smart Business Owners Develop Creative Ideas for True Growth* was incubated during an Achiever's Circle weekend with Mark LeBlanc. It proves to Susan that guidance, encouragement and advice from other respected experts is the key to everyone's success. DIY is not for those who are truly committed to success.

On a personal note, Susan is the proud 'mom' to a young Bernese Mountain Dog, Gabe. Gabe is Bernese Mountain Dog number 5. Susan says that when she brought him home, she was profoundly moved by realizing the cycle of love, loss and love again that is the familiar backdrop for our lives.

In the early years of her career, Susan had a varied and interesting series of experiences. Following college graduation she was a caseworker for New York City's Department of Child Welfare. She moved on to work for the long-time fashion shoe company I. Miller. It was at I. Miller that the appeal of business, with all its challenges and risks, began to build. After a couple of years she went to the University of Bridgeport, CT to study for her MBA. She dove deep into Finance and Economics, becoming what the Chair of the Department of Finance and Economics called his best student in 20 years of teaching. Following the awarding of her degree, she was hired as an Adjunct Professor of Finance and Economics, a position she held and loved for 5 years.

Simultaneously with graduate school, Susan served as the Director of Development for a community science and arts museum and offered financial advising services to young women. She also invested in real estate.

The more recent part of Susan's bio is the topic of Chapter Two in this book.

MY PHILOSOPHY: SINGULAR FOCUS

Endless demands on their attention: that's the life of too many Owners and CEOs.

Consequently, one common response is to try to improve prioritization, time management or delegation. The thinking goes that if you could just manage your time better, set priorities better, or delegate more, you would be able to improve every corner of the business. Time after time, people realize these efforts do not work.

The opposite and superior response is developing an extreme degree of focus. What I call Singular Focus^{SM}. It sets leaders and their companies up for long-term success. Singular Focus^{SM} directs your full attention to the 6 facets of business that most profoundly impact revenue and profit growth for every company. As a result of the deep dives into each Focus Area, the CEOs and Owners have more energy and space to turn their attention to other important parts of their life and future instead of being mired in the relentless present.

The 6 Focus Areas deserving Singular Focus^{SM} have a *profound and self-sustaining impact on your topline revenue and your bottom line profit.*

THE 6 FOCUS AREAS

- **Maximize Best Buyer Revenue:** Properly understand who your best buyers are, cultivate and nurture them, and they will eagerly buy your high-value, high-profit offerings.

- **Maximize Topline Revenue:** Provide a range of offerings for a range of buyers to increase revenue. Look at every single detail, large and small, that leads to money coming in the door.

- **Maximize Per Employee Revenue:** People buy from other people, not companies. Therefore, invest in your people and every other investment you make will be amplified.

- **Maximize Sales Cycle Speed:** Shorten the time from inquiry to payment. The buyer and the seller are both better off with a shorter, higher-speed sales cycle.

- **Maximize Owner Wellbeing:** Improve these five factors to maximize owner wellbeing: 1) increasing revenue; 2) adjusting the owner's mindset and daily activities; 3) identifying internal champions; 4) engaging outside experts; 5) recognizing economic conditions.

- **Maximize Owner Wealth:** Owner wealth allows you design the life you want and it is your return for all the years of risk you've taken.

The business environment is constantly changing. Susan Trivers is the Singular Focus^{SM} expert who can help you create dramatic revenue growth efficiently and satisfyingly. Connect the Focus Areas and design the future as you wish.

Learn more about Susan and Trivers Consulting Group at www.susantrivers.com.

Take a minute to call Susan Trivers to learn how Singular Focus^{SM} will help your company. 703-790-1424.

SPEAKING

Susan Trivers does more to capitalize on current buyers, current offerings and current employees than any advisor consulting with companies up to $20 million annual revenue.

When she speaks, Susan shares it all with her audiences of active business owners.

Her topics include the following:

Tinker: How Smart Business Owners Develop Creative Ideas for True Growth

True Growth is sustainable growth, built on a existing foundation that puts current customers and clients first. Learn Susan's Three-T Model to improve and innovate what you've already got out in the market. You'll learn how hunches, experiments and tinkering can generate 10, 20, even 30% growth for very low cost or investment.

Six Weeks to Robust, Awesome, Dynamic: Singular Focus^{SM} Quick Start, Quick Results

Singular Focus^{SM} is Susan's unique approach to maximizing the six outcomes that add up to dramatic, repeatable growth and boost owner wealth and well-being.

With Susan's Six Week Quick Start, business owners learn to implement one powerful tactic in each of the six Focus Areas and enjoy quick wins. Susan's pro tip: do a six-week sequence and then repeat. Each new round of six weeks builds on the success of the round before. The sky is the limit with this sequential approach to growth.

How to Capitalize on Your Current Buyers, Offerings and Employees

Susan is known for her deep expertise and extensive creativity when it comes to building a business on the foundation of current buyers, current offerings and current employees. Research shows that the vast majority of companies ignore or disappoint people who have already bought from them. They lose to other companies or to forgetfulness, inertia or disinterest. This costs them hundreds of millions of dollars.

Audiences get insight into Susan's innovative GO Curve concept for segmenting and aligning buyers, offerings and marketing efforts. This segmenting and aligning ensures that the right products and services are developed for existing buyers and that marketing efforts are making the intended impact on their recipients.

INVITE SUSAN TO YOUR NEXT EVENT

When you are planning an event for business owners, be sure to include Susan Trivers. She's a long time, experienced speaker who puts the audience first and works with organizers to ensure her content excites the audience and sends them home with great value.

Susan will customize the length of her speeches to work with your schedule. She includes audience participation to help with enjoyment in the moment and retention for the long term. She offers pre-and post-conference options to improve the audience's likelihood of actualizing her ideas.

Susan welcomes all inquiries. Please call 703-790-1424 or write susan@susantrivers.com

SUSANISMS

"Hunches are not accidents. They are hard earned, the result of years of work and lessons learned. They don't come from out of the blue, they bubble up from a place of knowledge and expertise within. Embrace your hunches; take action."

"The single biggest barrier to success is failure of imagination. It is not lack of money, lack of courage or lack of support from others."

"My work has been profoundly improved by changing how I think about failure. I used to think "I tried this and I failed." That was the end of the story. I realized that this shortchanges us. The full statement should be "I tried X and I failed to achieve the outcome Y that I was aiming for." The difference is that you can then go on to say: "I learned a lot more about X than I ever knew before. I also have some ideas about how to do X better, or to do Z instead.""

"Just because you'll never be the size of Apple or Space-x and Tesla, doesn't mean you shouldn't learn from them. It's not about actual techniques (e.g., 100s of engineers and designers working on the iPhone). It's about having intense and singular focus on one particular effort for a sustained period of time that will dramatically change your business."

"True growth happens when the smart business owner focuses on making it happen. It is all day, every day, month after month and year after year."

"What I know about tinkering: nothing is ever perfect (ever!) and that is not the goal of tinkering. The goal of tinkering is improvement, creativity and innovation; opening up to what is unknown to you at the start."

"Experiments always teach lessons that your routine cannot."

"Go with your instinct or your gut. You've been around long enough to have plenty of lessons learned. They are giving you your hunches."

"Write a detailed plan with dates/times; persons/people responsible; discrete action steps; data collection. Be prepared to course correct when need. Flexibility is a virtue."

"The personal touch means more than anything."

"How you use your time reflects your priorities."

"I believe hourly billing is destructive to relationships. Value based fees build relationships."

TRIVERS CONSULTING GROUP MISSION VISION AND VALUES

Mission: to help owner-led companies capitalize on their current assets-- current buyers, current offerings and current employees-- for maximum revenue and profit.

Vision: Every business owner builds value and wealth as soon as possible and for as long as possible.

Values: Honesty, integrity, high value.

PRINCIPLES FOR CAPITALIZING ON CURRENT ASSETS

Singular Focus^{SM} on current buyers and current offerings; perfect alignment of offerings with buyers; increase value and earn revenue commensurate with that value.

Invest 80% of your marketing efforts on current buyers; 20% on attracting new buyers. Keep track and measure this. Don't guess.

Cultivate and nurture current buyers with tactics aligned with the buyer's value to your company.

See every employee in every role as a contributor to revenue and profit. Ask how you can ensure they contribute, do not assume due to their job title that they can't.

Never confuse busyness with achieving outcomes.

Achieve your outcomes no matter what.

Learn to say "no" without hesitation. And mean it. And repeat as necessary.

The more you capitalize on your current assets, the more opportunities you will have to continue doing that. Today's foundation will not be your foundation a month or a year from now. Keep building.

Don't suffer from a failure of imagination that there is a better way.

NOTES

NOTES

NOTES

NOTES

NOTES

NOTES

NOTES

NOTES

NOTES

NOTES

NOTES

NOTES

NOTES

NOTES

NOTES

NOTES

Made in the USA
Columbia, SC
12 July 2018